YOUNG ZOOLOGIST
CAPYBARA

A FIRST FIELD GUIDE TO THE BIGGEST
RODENT IN THE WORLD

CONTENTS

HELLO, YOUNG ZOOLOGIST!

Welcome to the world of capybaras! My name is Julia and I am a scientist from Argentina, a country in South America where capybaras can be found. I have been studying capybaras for years and can't wait to share everything I've learned with you. Do you want to know more about these cute and funny animals? Then let's explore their world together!

DR. JULIA MATA

FACT FILE

SCIENTIFIC NAME
Hydrochoerus hydrochaeris

CLASS
Mammal

FAMILY
Rodent

EATS
Grass and aquatic plants

SPECIES
There are two different species of capybara:

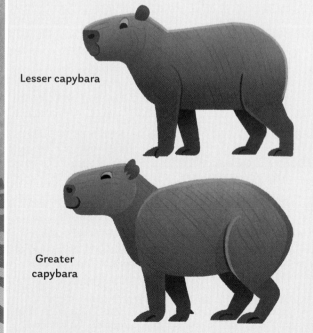

Lesser capybara

Greater capybara

SIZE AND WEIGHT
Capybaras weigh around 110 lb (50 kg), which is the same as two eight-year-old children! This makes them the largest rodents in the world. They are 5,000 times bigger than the smallest rodent, the northern pygmy mouse.

WHERE ARE THEY FOUND?
East of the Andes mountains in every South American country but Chile (the dark green area of the map)

STATUS
Least concern

LIFESPAN
4–10 years

BEFORE YOU GET STARTED

1 RAIN BOOTS
Capybaras live near water, so the right boots can help you walk through the muddy ground. Rain boots can also protect you from snakes that may be hiding in the grass!

2 BUG SPRAY
Heat plus water equals mosquitoes, and there tends to be a lot of them where you find capybaras! Mosquitoes can carry diseases, so it is important to wear insect repellent.

3 SUNSCREEN AND HAT
Capybaras tend to live in hot, sunny places. A wide-brimmed hat will help keep you cool, while sunscreen is essential to protect your skin from sunburn.

4 CAMERA TRAP
These special cameras are left in the wild to take pictures of animals when humans are not around. The photos help show us which animals are there and how they behave.

To study capybaras you have to go and visit them in their natural habitat. They live in warm and wet areas, so it is important that you are well prepared. You will need special equipment and clothing. Let's see what you need to pack!

5 NOTEBOOK AND PEN

Like any good scientist, you will need to collect information when you're in the field. You should keep a spiral notebook and a pen to write down all of your observations.

6 TAPE MEASURE AND FANNY PACK

In the field, a fanny pack will be your best friend (apart from the capybaras!). You can use it to store things you need to grab fast, like a tape measure to check sizes and distances.

7 CONTAINERS TO COLLECT SAMPLES

To study capybaras, you will need to collect samples in containers. You can collect the plants they eat as well as samples of their poop to take back to the lab for further study!

MEET THE CAPYBARA

PROTECTIVE FUR

Capybara fur is brown or reddish in color and consists of long, coarse hairs. Their thick hair protects them from the sun, skin parasites, and getting hurt by thorns and branches.

WEBBED FEET

Capybaras have webbed feet, just like frogs! The bits of skin between their toes make capybaras great swimmers. They often use the water as a way to escape when they feel threatened or scared.

Capybaras are funny-looking animals. They are related to mice and beavers, but they have no tail and they are much bigger than you would expect. There is a lot to learn about their bodies—let's take a closer look!

YE-SPY

A capybara's eyes are located at the top of its head on either side. This gives the capybara a good range of vision when on land and allows it to keep its eyes above the water when swimming.

SUPER SNIFFERS

A capybara's nose is near the top of its head so it can breathe while in the water. Capybaras have a great sense of smell, which they use to identify each other.

CHOPPERS

Capybaras' teeth never stop growing! The front teeth are long and used to cut grass. They sometimes bite each other to defend their territory.

NASAL GLAND

This special gland on the top of a capybara's nose is much bigger and more visible on male capybaras. It is a helpful way for us to identify which capybaras are male or female. Capybaras use this gland to mark their territory, because the oil it makes has a strong smell.

THE FAMILY

Capybaras are members of the rodent family. This group includes mice, rats, hamsters, and beavers. On these pages you will meet some of the rodents most closely related to capybaras. It's time for a family reunion!

AGOUTI

Agoutis live in Central and South America and some Caribbean islands, mainly in forests and grasslands. They eat fruits, roots, and leaves—often making holes in the ground to hide seeds to eat later on! Their front paws are able to hold their food.

GUINEA PIG

Guinea pigs are originally from the Andes mountains in South America. They were domesticated by the local people as a source of meat, but they are now more common as pets.

ROCK CAVY

These animals live in dry and rocky areas of Brazil, where they eat seeds and leaves. They live in groups and are most active at the beginning or end of the day.

NUTRIA

Nutrias are from South America, but they have also been taken by people to other continents. They are large rodents who munch on grasses and aquatic vegetation.

CHINCHILLA

Chinchillas live in colonies in the Andes mountains, eating leaves, seeds, and fruits. Chinchillas have soft and warm fur that helps them to survive high up in the mountains.

CAPYBARA HABITATS

PALM SAVANNA

Capybaras are always found near freshwater, but they also need shade and protection. Areas like palm savannas—with grasses, bushes, and palms next to wetlands or streams—are perfect places to live.

TREE SAVANNA

Tree savannas also have grasses and bushes but have larger trees like the African savannas you see in nature documentaries.

FORESTS

Capybaras can be found in forests and rainforests that have patches of grass going along a river, stream, or swamp.

It might surprise you to find out that capybaras can thrive in a range of different habitats. They live in parts of South America that include forests, wetlands, and savannas. These adaptable creatures can even be found near human settlements!

CAMERA TRAPS

To learn where capybaras are we can look for images of them taken by camera traps. Scientists put many of these cameras out in the wild. They take photos every time they detect movement in front of them.

DINNER IS SERVED

VEGETARIANS

Most of a capybara's diet consists of different types of grasses, but they will also eat plants that grow in water. They can be very picky and prefer soft and yummy plants, but they are less fussy in the dry season when it's harder to find food.

Grasses

Pickerelweed

Capybaras love to eat! They spend a lot of their time standing, sitting, or even lying down while munching on vegetation. They only eat plants, with one very curious exception...

DON'T TRY THIS AT HOME

Believe it or not, capybaras eat their own poop! They only do this in the mornings—directly from their butts. Eating their food for a second time helps them to better digest the nutrients from the plants they eat.

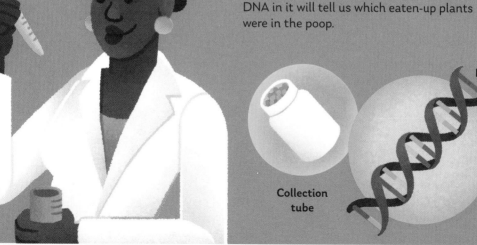

THE CLUE'S IN THE POOP

To study which plants capybaras eat, we can collect their poop and study it in a lab. The DNA in it will tell us which eaten-up plants were in the poop.

DNA

Collection tube

CAPYBARA LAWNS

When capybaras eat grass, they like to focus on certain areas. They use their teeth to cut the grass, creating patches with tasty short grass that other animals can also use.

Never underestimate a capybara! Despite their cute appearance, these rodents have a big impact on their ecosystems. They can change how an area looks and even how the other animals in the habitat use it.

FIRE BRIGADE

In savannas, fires are common and expected. However, the short-grass areas created by the capybaras don't go up in flames. As a result they can help stop the spread of the fires.

NO-CAPYBARA ZONES

To study the effects of capybaras on the vegetation of an area, scientists make fenced zones that capybaras can't enter. With time, the size and type of plants will change when there are no capybaras to chomp them up!

WALLOWING AROUND

By constantly sitting in a certain spot, capybaras create holes, or wallows, that fill with water. They love to lie in them on warm days—and other animals like to use them too!

A DAY IN THE LIFE

SWIMMING AWAY FROM PREDATORS

Capybaras are food for many of the carnivores (meat-eaters) in their habitat. This means they need to be on constant alert in case a predator such as a jaguar appears. To escape, they will often make use of their super swimming skills.

Capybaras may look super chilled out, but don't be fooled! These animals have plenty to do each day to keep them busy. Would you like to be a capybara for 24 hours?

SCENT MARKING

Capybaras are territorial animals. They mark their territories with smells from the glands they have above their nose and between their back legs. This way other capybaras know who runs the joint!

GIVE ME A HUG

In areas with chilly winters, capybaras huddle close together to keep warm during the coldest times of the day. While cozy, this huddling means it's easier for harmful skin parasites to pass from one capybara to another.

BARKING

Capybaras can make several different noises. When they want to tell others about possible threats they make a sound similar to a bark, which tells all the capybaras to run away!

STRONGER TOGETHER

SHARING THE LOAD

Living in groups has a lot of benefits for capybaras. It allows them to share responsibilities, such as keeping an eye out for threats and taking care of the pups.

Capybaras live in groups of 5 to 20 adults in savannas but only 2 to 3 adults in forests.

Group living is an important part of the life of capybaras. Hanging out in a big family clan keeps them safer from threats and helps them to defend their territory from outsiders. They may sometimes fight but it is never for long!

HOME SWEET HOME

The territory of the group is marked and defended by the males. Prized areas include grassy patches next to fresh water, and areas on higher ground where capybaras can stay safe if there is flooding.

WHO'S BOSS?

In a group of capybaras there tends to be one dominant male, but there are also other males in the clan. The hierarchy of the males is set through "fights," which mostly consist of them chasing each other!

LIFE CYCLE

1 MOM AND DAD
Capybaras love water, so when a male and a female pair up they will mate in the water. They can reproduce all year long, however, usually all of the females in a group are ready to mate at around the same time.

2 BUNS IN THE OVEN
Pregnancy lasts five months. Female capybaras can carry up to eight pups in their tummies, though the average is around four. During pregnancy, the mom's belly becomes big and round, looking like it might almost touch the ground!

3 HAPPY BIRTHDAY
The pups are born with hair and can walk hours after birth. They can even climb on top of the adults to avoid the water! Within a group, all of the females give birth within the same two weeks.

Capybaras have a fast life cycle. They are mature enough to have their own pups before they're two years old, and they can have one or two litters of pups a year. This is one of the reasons why capybara populations are doing so well!

4 TEAMWORK MAKES THE DREAM WORK

The females help each other with the nursing of the pups. Since the pups are all around the same age, they are able to drink milk from any of the mothers.

5 THEY GROW UP SO FAST

The pups grow, and after four months they stop drinking milk and start only eating plants. They will stay together—and never far from an adult—for several more months until they become adults themselves.

WATCH OUT!

DEADLY PREDATORS

Jaguars are the largest cat in the Americas and, like pumas, are able to hunt and eat a full-grown capybara. Caimans and black vultures are common in capybara habitats and can hunt the pups. Vultures are scavengers, so they will also happily eat carcasses left behind by other predators.

Jaguar

Caiman

HUMAN THREAT

Humans hunt capybaras for their meat. They also use their skin to create leather, which can be used to make gloves, shoes, and bags. Humans are also responsible for damaging the habitat capybaras live in by cutting down trees and farming the land.

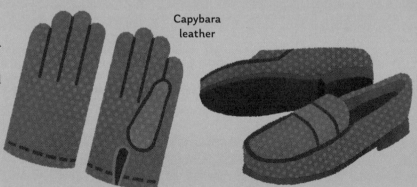

Capybara leather

Capybaras are not endangered animals but they do face threats—especially when they are young. From animal predators to humans, a capybara must always keep its eye out for danger.

Black vultures

Puma

PARASITES

A lot of wild animals carry diseases and parasites, which can make them sick. Capybaras tend to have a lot of ticks in their skin, tiny parasites in their blood, and worms in their tummy.

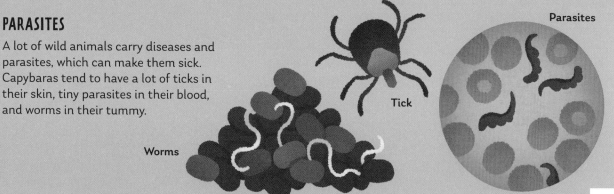

Parasites

Tick

Worms

FRIENDS FOREVER

Capybaras are friendly animals that tend to get along with their neighbors. However, they do have some friends they are closer to than others. Here we will learn about their best friends: birds!

HORSEFLIES

Horseflies are not friends to capybaras. They have stronger mouthparts than normal flies and can bite large animals like capybaras. They drink their blood and can transmit parasites to them. Some birds remove them from the backs of capybaras. Thanks, guys!

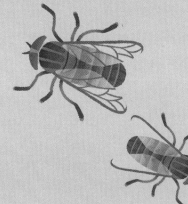

FEATHERED FRIENDS

If you ever see a capybara in the wild, it is only a matter of time before you see a bird on them! Some birds, like the cowbird and the cattle tyrant, eat the bugs that fly up when capybaras walk through grass. Other birds, like the caracara and the jacana, have a mutually beneficial relationship with capybaras. They stand on capybaras and eat the parasites that are on their skin!

RHINO AND OXPECKER

Another famous example of a mutually beneficial relationship between a big mammal and a bird is the rhino and the oxpecker. These birds eat ticks, insects, and parasites that are on the rhino's skin.

MARSH DEER

Marsh deer are the biggest deer in South America. They live in wetlands and marshes.

BIRDS

A lot of different birds live alongside capybaras. Some interact with them, while others benefit from the capybara lawn-mowing service!

NEIGHBORS

We know capybaras like birds, but that's not all. They will be friendly with a whole range of species, including some that eat them! Let's meet some of the other creatures capybaras hang out with in the wild.

RHEA

Rheas are some of the biggest birds in South America, standing at around the height of a teenager! They can't fly but are good runners.

GIANT ANTEATERS

These funny-looking animals can be up to 6 ½ ft (2 m) long. They eat ants and termites using their very long and thin tongues.

CAIMAN

These relatives of crocodiles like to eat capybaras, but you will also often see them sunbathing together!

TURTLES

Capybaras share streams and lakes with freshwater turtles. Like capybaras, they have webbed feet.

GLOSSARY

Carnivore
An animal that eats meat.

Colony
A group of animals of the same species that live together in the same place.

DNA
Information inside cells that determines how an animal or plant will look and function.

Ecosystem
Living things and their environment and how they all interact with one another.

Endangered
Used to describe a species that faces consistent threats and has lost many individuals because of them.

Habitat
An area that has all of the things a particular species needs to survive and reproduce.

Mate
The act performed by a male and a female of the same species that creates a pup or baby.

Parasite
A species that uses another animal to survive, often causing it harm in the process.

Predator
An animal that kills and eats other animals.

Prey
An animal that is killed and eaten by other animals.

Pup
The term used to describe a baby capybara.

Rodent
A group of related animals with front teeth that never stop growin This group includes mice, hamster beavers, and capybaras.

Savanna
An ecosystem that is a mix of trees and grasslands.

Scavenger
An animal that eats the meat from animals that are already dead.

Territory
Part of the habitat that a group of animals of the same species defend and live in together.

INDEX

This has been a

NEON 🦑 SQUID

production

To my friends and family for supporting me and encouraging my love for capybaras.

To my parents for storing capybara poop samples under their roof since 2018.

To my abuela Elida, who after watching my PhD defense commented: there were a lot of capybaras in it.

Author: Dr. Julia Mata
Illustrator: Greco Westermann

Design: Collaborate Agency
US Editor: Jill Freshney
Proofreader: Joseph Barnes

Copyright © 2024
St. Martin's Press
120 Broadway, New York,
NY 10271

Created for St. Martin's Press
by Neon Squid
The Smithson, 6 Briset Street,
London, EC1M 5NR

EU representative: Macmillan
Publishers Ireland Ltd,
1st Floor, The Liffey Trust Centre,
117–126 Sheriff Street Upper,
Dublin 1, D01 YC43

10 9 8 7 6 5 4 3 2 1

Library of Congress Cataloging-in-Publication Data is available.

Printed and bound in Guangdong, China by Leo Paper Products Ltd.

ISBN: 978-1-684-49512-2

Published in October 2024.

www.neonsquidbooks.com